#BESTIE

BESTIE

Summersdale Publishers Ltd
46 West Street
Chichester
West Sussex
PO19 1RP
UK

www.summersdale.com

Printed and bound in the Czech Republic

ISBN: 978-1-78685-201-4

Substantial discounts on bulk quantities of Summersdale books are available to corporations, professional associations and other organisations. For details contact general enquiries: telephone: +44 (0) 1243 771107 or email: enquiries@summersdale.com.

bestie

summersdale

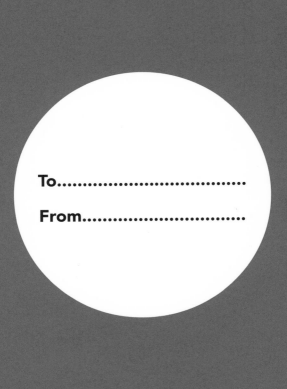

To.....................................

From.................................

DEAR BESTIE, I HONESTLY DON'T KNOW

WHAT I'D DO WITHOUT YOU

True friends are like diamonds – bright, beautiful, valuable and always in style.

Nicole Richie

Women are the largest untapped reservoir of talent in the world.

Hillary Clinton

Some girls are just born with glitter in their veins

NO ONE CAN MAKE YOU FEEL INFERIOR WITHOUT YOUR CONSENT.

Eleanor Roosevelt

Never give up, for that is just the place and time that the tide will turn.

Harriet Beecher Stowe

**If a woman
is sufficiently
ambitious, determined
and gifted – there is
practically nothing
she can't do.**

Helen Lawrenson

ONE GIRL CAN MAKE A DIFFERENCE

TWO GIRLS CAN CHANGE THE WORLD

= **BEST
FRIEND
GOALS**

I like you
because we hate
the same stuff

ONE IS NOT BORN, BUT RATHER BECOMES, A WOMAN.

Simone de Beauvoir

You only live once, but if you do it right, once is enough.

Mae West

**You grow up the day
you have the first real
laugh at yourself.**

Ethel Barrymore

#Babe

A LOT OF PEOPLE ARE AFRAID TO SAY WHAT THEY WANT. THAT'S WHY THEY DON'T GET WHAT THEY WANT.

Madonna

SHE'S BRIGHT LIKE GLITTER AND BUBBLY LIKE CHAMPAGNE...

AND SHARP
LIKE BARBED
WIRE

Wherever
we are, it is our
friends that make
our world.

Henry Drummond

I think that
sometimes
being fearless is
having fears but
jumping anyway.

Taylor Swift

Everything in my life, every answer in my life, every opportunity is always my decision.

Nicki Minaj

In my moments
of doubt I've told
myself firmly – if
not me, who? If
not now, when?

Emma Watson

We're not afraid to sparkle

A FRIEND IS ONE
THAT KNOWS
YOU AS YOU
ARE, ACCEPTS
WHAT YOU HAVE
BECOME AND
ALLOWS YOU
TO GROW.

Anonymous

Nothing is better than a friend, unless it is a friend with chocolate.

Linda Grayson

Girl squad

PRINCESS?

NO, LADY:
QUEEN

A girl doesn't need
anyone who doesn't
need her.

Marilyn Monroe

WHEN A WOMAN BECOMES HER OWN BEST FRIEND

LIFE IS EASIER.

Diane von Fürstenberg

**Believe in
your inner
Beyoncé**

Some souls just understand each other upon meeting.

N. R. Hart

A true friend is
someone who lets
you have total
freedom to be
yourself.

Jim Morrison

YOU CAN'T DO IT ALONE... **OTHER PEOPLE AND OTHER PEOPLE'S IDEAS ARE OFTEN BETTER THAN YOUR OWN.**

Amy Poehler

I HOPE WE'RE FRIENDS UNTIL WE DIE....

**THEN I HOPE
WE STAY
GHOST
FRIENDS
AND WALK
THROUGH
WALLS
SCARING THE
HELL OUT OF
PEOPLE**

I embrace
mistakes. They
make you
who you are.

Beyoncé

If you really want to fly, harness your power to your passion.

Oprah Winfrey

I'm not interested
in money, I just want
to be wonderful.

Marilyn Monroe

You are
awesome

Be strong, love and believe in yourself.

Emma Watson

DON'T GET BITTER, JUST GET BETTER.

Alyssa Edwards

#winning

**If you obey
all the rules,
you miss all
the fun.**

Katharine Hepburn

1 PLANET,
7 CONTINENTS,
HUNDREDS OF
COUNTRIES...

AND I HAD THE PRIVILEGE OF MEETING YOU

A woman is like a teabag – you can't tell how strong she is until she gets into hot water.

Anonymous

IGNORE
THE HATERS

The most courageous act is still to think for yourself. Aloud.

Coco Chanel

Dream crazy big

My best friend is the one who brings out the best in me.

Henry Ford

THERE ARE TWO WAYS OF SPREADING LIGHT:
TO BE THE CANDLE OR THE MIRROR THAT REFLECTS IT.

Edith Wharton

YOU ONLY
LIVE ONCE,

SO YOU MIGHT AS WELL SLAY!

Only your real friends will tell you when your face is dirty.

Sicilian proverb

Chin up –
we've got this

The most
beautiful discovery
true friends make
is that they can grow
separately without
growing apart.

Elisabeth Foley

Best friends
are hard to
find because
the very best is
already mine!

I think women are foolish to pretend they are equal to men, they are far superior and always have been.

William Golding

THE IMPORTANT THING IS NOT WHAT THEY THINK OF ME, BUT WHAT I THINK OF THEM.

Queen Victoria

A girl should
be two things:
who and what
she wants.

Coco Chanel

I don't want
other people to
decide who I am.
I want to decide
that for myself.

Emma Watson

THANK YOU
FOR BEING

MY
UNBIOLOGICAL
SISTER

Own who
you are

IT'S EASIER TO BE BRAVE WHEN YOU'RE NOT ALONE.

Amy Poehler

Soul sister

**No one has
ever been able to
tell me I couldn't do
something because
I was a girl.**

Anne Hathaway

Happiness and confidence are the prettiest things you can wear.

Taylor Swift

NO ONE WILL EVER BE AS ENTERTAINED BY US AS US

**OUR LAUGHS?
LIMITLESS**

**OUR
MEMORIES?
COUNTLESS**

OUR
FRIENDSHIP?
THE BEST!

Doubt is a killer. You just have to know who you are and what you stand for.

Jennifer Lopez

Say yes, and you'll figure it out afterwards.

Tina Fey

True friendship comes when silence between two people is comfortable.

David Tyson Gentry

We can do
anything and
nothing,
and still have
the best time

The love that comes with friendship is the underlying facet of a happy life.

Chelsea Handler

WE R 2 FAB

4 YOU

Don't be like anyone else. Find your voice, your script, your rhythms.

Jill Soloway

It's the friends
you can call up
at 4 a.m.
that matter.

Marlene Dietrich

I THOUGHT
I WAS
NORMAL....

UNTIL I MET MY BEST FRIEND

You're my
#BOSSBABE

IT IS NOT SO
MUCH OUR
FRIENDS' HELP
THAT HELPS US
AS THE
CONFIDENT
KNOWLEDGE
THAT THEY
WILL HELP US.

Epicurus

Too glam
to give
a damn

**You have what it takes
to be a victorious,
independent,
fearless woman.**

Tyra Banks

Always be a first-rate version of yourself, instead of a second-rate version of somebody else.

Judy Garland

IF YOU THINK YOU'RE TOO SMALL TO HAVE AN IMPACT, TRY GOING TO BED WITH A MOSQUITO.

Anita Roddick

BOYS ARE WHATEVER,

BEST FRIENDS
ARE FOREVER

Sassy

since birth

Girls should never be afraid to be smart.

Emma Watson

Don't waste your energy trying to educate or change opinions... Do your thing and don't care if they like it.

Tina Fey

You can't
be afraid of what
people are going
to say, because you're
never going to make
everyone happy.

Selena Gomez

I say if I'm beautiful.
I say if I'm strong.
You will not determine
my story – I will.

Amy Schumer

NEVER DULL YOUR SHINE FOR SOMEBODY ELSE.

Tyra Banks

**Your vibe
attracts
your tribe**

When someone
tells you that you
can't, turn around
and say 'watch me'.

Anonymous

SHE BELIEVED
SHE COULD

SO SHE DID

A queen is not afraid to fail. Failure is another stepping stone to greatness.

Oprah Winfrey

**IF YOU FALL,
I WILL ALWAYS
BE THERE TO
PICK YOU
UP... AFTER
I'VE FINISHED
LAUGHING!**

The question isn't who is going to let me, it's who is going to stop me.

Ayn Rand

We call upon our sisters around the world to be brave – to embrace the strength within themselves and realise their full potential.

Malala Yousafzai

The thing women have yet to learn is nobody gives you power. You just take it.

Roseanne Barr

I AM NOT AFRAID;

I WAS BORN TO DO THIS.

Joan of Arc

WE'LL ALWAYS BE BEST FRIENDS

BECAUSE YOU KNOW TOO MUCH

=GIRLPOWER

Rare as is true love, true friendship is rarer.

Jean de La Fontaine

I figure, if a girl
wants to be a legend,
she should just go
ahead and be one.

Calamity Jane

Above all,
be the heroine
of your life,
not the victim.

Nora Ephron

Women have been trained to speak softly and carry a lipstick. Those days are over.

Bella Abzug

YOU KNOW HOW CRAZY I AM, BUT YOU'RE STILL HAPPY TO BE SEEN WITH ME IN PUBLIC

Nothing can dim the light which shines from within.

Maya Angelou

Keep your friends close. Buy your enemies something cool.

Lena Dunham

BEST FRIEND
IS A PROMISE

NOT A LABEL

A best friend is
like a four-leaf clover:
hard to find, and
lucky to have.

Sarah Jessica Parker

TRUE FRIENDS ARE THOSE WHO REALLY KNOW YOU BUT LOVE YOU ANYWAY.

Edna Buchanan

**The best mirror
is a friend's eye.**

Gaelic proverb

I'm a big believer
in accepting yourself
the way you are and
not really worrying
about it.

Jennifer Lawrence

I think about my best
friendship... as like
a great romance of
my young life.

Lena Dunham

I ONLY
ROLL WITH
GODDESSES

GROW OLD GRACEFULLY? NO CHANCE...

WE'LL BE TEARING UP THE NURSING HOME TOGETHER

Don't be
afraid to speak
up for yourself.
Keep fighting for
your dreams!

Gabby Douglas

I don't care what
is written about
me so long as it
isn't true.

Dorothy Parker

Love you, bestie

Attitude is everything.

Diane von Fürstenberg

Female friendships that work are relationships in which women help each other belong to themselves.

Louise Bernikow

PARTNERS
IN CRIME

You're only
young once,
but you can
be immature
forever.

Germaine Greer

You're pretty much my favourite person in the history of the world... ever

KEEP CALM

AND LOVE
YOUR BFF

Any day spent with you is my favourite day. So today is my new favourite day.

A. A. Milne

YAAAAAAAASSSS
SSSSSSSSSSS
SSSSSSSS!

Each friend represents a world in us.

Anaïs Nin

True friendship resists time, distance and silence.

Isabel Allende

Always remember you're unique, just like everyone else.

Alison Boulter

IF YOU HAVEN'T LEARNED THE MEANING OF FRIENDSHIP, YOU REALLY HAVEN'T LEARNED ANYTHING.

Muhammad Ali

YOU'RE
THE BEST

OF THE
BESTIES!

#squadgoals

Sometimes you just have to put on lip gloss and pretend to be psyched.

Mindy Kaling

Other women who are killing it should motivate you, thrill you, challenge you and inspire you.

Taylor Swift

There's power
in looking silly
and not caring
that you do.

Amy Poehler

Be cool,
hunny bunny

USE EACH INTERACTION TO BE THE BEST, MOST POWERFUL VERSION OF YOURSELF.

Marianne Williamson

SURROUND YOURSELF WITH THE THINGS YOU LOVE...

**DISCARD
THE REST**

NAMASTE,
BESTIE

If you're interested in finding out more about our books, find us on Facebook at **Summersdale Publishers** and follow us on Twitter at **@Summersdale**.

www.summersdale.com